GW01606968

For children ages 3-7

Learns the Value of
Helping and Cooperation

A Division of GL Publications
Ventura, California U.S.A.

Ethel Barrett

Clay art by David Gaddy

Published by Regal Books
A Division of GL Publications
Ventura, California 93006
Printed in U.S.A.

Library of Congress Cataloging-in-Publication Date applied for

Puff was indeed proud of himself. And he had every right to be, for he had just finished building a tunnel that led down to the most secret part of the entire community, to the place where the food was stored. Oh, didn't I tell you? Puff was an ant.

In his head he had eyes to see with and
feelers to feel with, and jaws to eat with
and grab ahold of things.
He was sort of skinny in the middle, but on the *other* end
of him was his stomach. Actually, he had two stomachs.
One stomach he stored food in for himself,
and the other stomach was his "sharing" stomach.
That's where he stored the food to feed to other ants.
He would *squeeze* and *squeeze* until the food got up
to his mouth, and then he'd drop it off for the other ants to eat.
(Actually it's called the social stomach.)
And he had six legs to run around with.
And could he ever run!
Well, you can see why
Puff felt important.

Now, usually where the ants live—
it's called their colony— is all underground
where you can't see them.
But Puff didn't live underground.
He lived in an ant palace and it looked like this.
Puff didn't *even* *know* that he lived
in an ant palace until one day—
He made a sharp turn to the left
while he was digging—and bumped—
BONK!?!—smack into the glass wall
of the ant palace.

And there he saw—
CHILDREN staring him
right in the face.
A boy and a girl.
"Did you see that ant?"
the girl said. "He came
right up to the glass to visit
with us."
"Yeah," said the boy.
"He must like us."
The little girl moved up
closer. "He must be a very
important ant," she said.

Well! When Puff heard this, he uncrumpled his legs and backed up to the main tunnel to brag to all the other ants. It was there that he bumped into his cousin DIZZY. Dizzy was struggling in the tunnel with a huge chunk of food. They both stopped in their tracks, facing each other.

"I'm sure glad I bumped into you, Puff," Dizzy said.
"You can help me with this."
"No," Puff said,
"I can do it by myself."
"But we can BOTH do it
better TOGETHER, Puff."
"I'll do it, Dizzy, let me
do it. I'll do it myself."

And he tugged at the load until it fell to the ground. Dizzy was furious. "Do you know what's wrong with you, Puff?

Do you know why we all call you Puff?
Because you're STUCK-UP, that's why.
You're all puffed up.
You think you're more important than anybody else and you won't let anybody help you. You want to do everything all by yourself. That's why we call you Puff!"
he shouted.

Well, in the end, they managed to get the huge load down the tunnel. Puff was pulling and Dizzy was pushing. When they got the job done, you'd better believe that Puff bragged that he had done it all by himself. "I don't need anybody to help me. I don't need anybody to help me ever. I can do everything all by myself," he bragged.

But before he could say another word,
his whole world was turned upside down!
Fluff, the cat, had tipped over the ant palace,
and it had fallen off the table,
and all the sand had poured out—
all over the rug in the living room!
"Where am I?" Puff gasped. "Somebody help me.
All my tunnels are gone! I don't even
know where I am!"

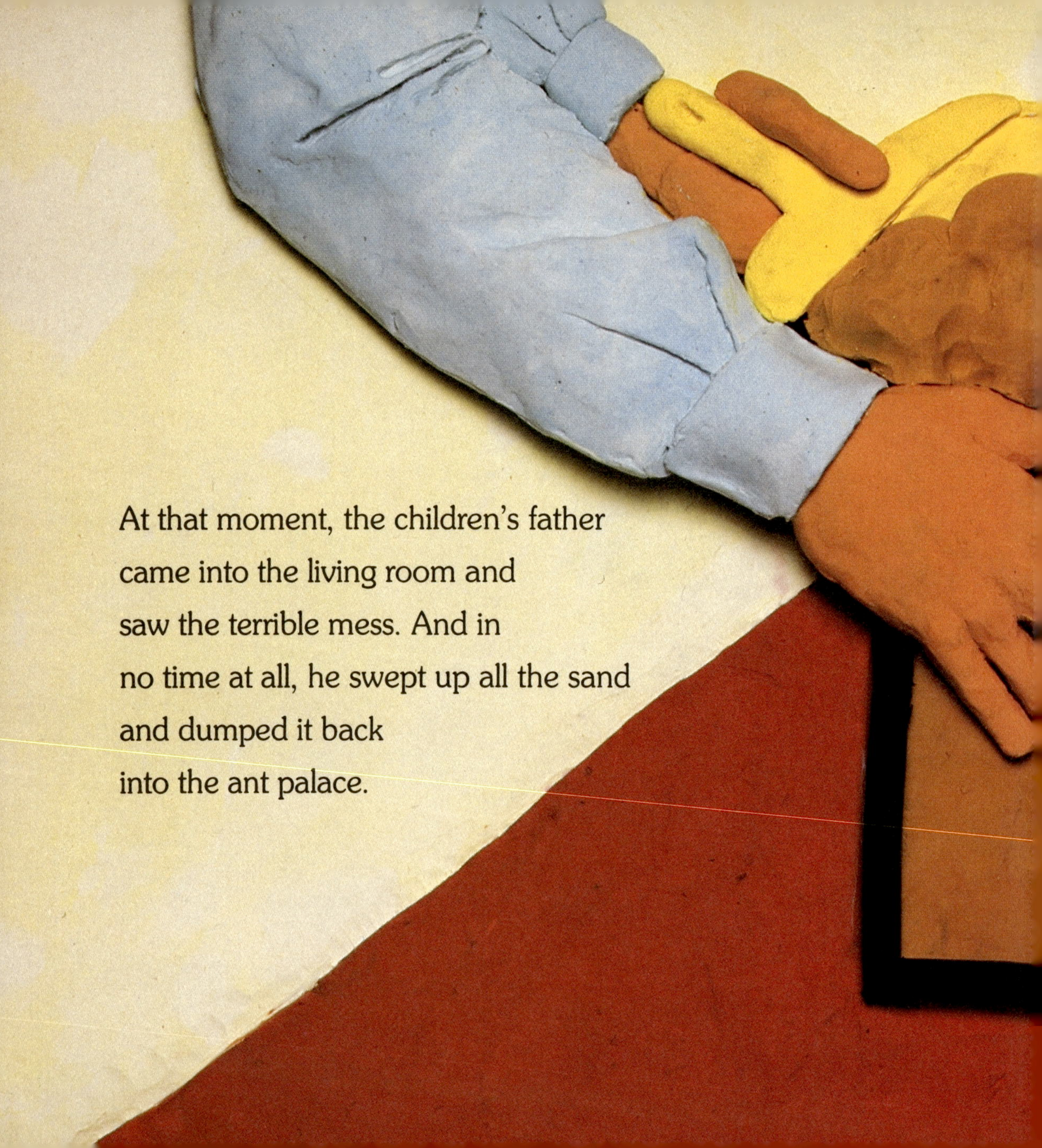

At that moment, the children's father came into the living room and saw the terrible mess. And in no time at all, he swept up all the sand and dumped it back into the ant palace.

Inside the ant palace, there was total confusion!
The beautiful ant colony had been totally destroyed.
The tunnels were gone, the rooms were gone,
EVERYTHING was gone! All the ants scurried
up to the top of the sand as best they could.
Puff found himself sitting up on the sand.
All the other ants were there, and right next to Puff—
was his cousin Dizzy.
"Everything's gone, Dizzy," Puff cried.
"EVERYTHING'S GONE.
What'll we do, Dizzy?
What'll we do?"

"There's only one thing we can do, Puff," Dizzy said. "We've got to start from scratch and build our colony all over again." Puff didn't notice, but for the first time in his life he did not say, "I can do it myself." Instead, he kept saying over and over again, "I'll help, I'll help."

So, all the ants got busy; they began to build tunnels, and they built their rooms all over again and they put everything back in its place.

And, from that moment on, Puff was the greatest
little helper that any ant could possibly be.
And all the other ants liked him now.
He had more friends than he could count.
Of course, they all still called him Puff,
'cause that was his name and
he was stuck with it.
But he never forgot
his lesson.

From that moment on, he never said, "I can do it by myself." No. Instead, he always said, "Hey, fella. Let me help you. We can both do it TOGETHER."

Just like the Bible says, "Each of you should look not only to your own interests, but also to the interests of others" Philippians 2:4 (*NIV*). It's important to care about other people and to work together as a TEAM.